Sonia Bompastor

A Trailblazer in Women's Football

Mike A. McGee

Copyright © 2024 by Mike A. McGee.

All rights reserved. No part of this publication may be replicated, disseminated, or transmitted in any form or by any means, including photocopying, recording, or other electronic or mechanical methods, without the prior written consent of the publisher, except in the case of brief excerpts embodied in critical reviews and specific other noncommercial uses permitted by copyright law.

Table of Contents

Introduction

- Who Is Sonia Bompastor?
- Why She Matters in Women's Football

Chapter 1: Early Life and Background

- Childhood and Family
- First Steps into Football

Chapter 2. Professional Football Career

- Clubs She Played For
- Major Achievements and Awards
- Key Moments on the Field

Chapter 3. International Career with France

- Representing the French National Team

- Memorable Tournaments and Matches

Chapter 4. Transition to Coaching

- From Player to Manager

- Philosophy and Approach as a Coach

- Leading Olympique Lyonnais Féminin

Chapter 5. Leadership and Legacy

- Pioneering Roles in Women's Football

- Influence on Future Generations

Chapter 6. Personal Life and Interests

- Life Outside Football
- Balancing Career and Family

Chapter 7. Challenges and Resilience

- Overcoming Obstacles in Her Career
- Lessons Learned

Chapter 8. Impact on Women's Football

- Elevating the Sport's Visibility
- Advocating for Women's Rights in Sports

Chapter 9. Media and Public Presence

- Interviews, Documentaries, and Coverage

- Public Image and Influence

Chapter 10. Awards, Honors, and Recognitions

- National and International Acknowledgments

- Hallmarks of a Legendary Career

Chapter 11. Fun Facts and Lesser-Known Details

- Surprising Facts About Sonia Bompastor

- Behind-the-Scenes Stories

Chapter 12. Frequently Asked Questions (FAQs)

- Common Questions About Her Life and Career

Chapter 13. Quotes and Insights from Sonia Bompastor

- Inspirational Quotes
- Insights into Her Vision

Chapter 14. Timeline of Sonia Bompastor's Life

- Key Events from Birth to Present

Chapter 15. Conclusion

- Sonia Bompastor's Enduring Legacy
- The Future of Women's Football

Introduction

In the vibrant world of sports, few figures embody passion, resilience, and innovation quite like Sonia Bompastor. A name synonymous with excellence in women's football, Bompastor has carved an indelible legacy that resonates far beyond the pitch. Her story is not just one of personal triumph but a testament to the transformative power of determination, leadership, and vision in a sport traditionally overshadowed by its male counterpart.

Through her career as a player and a coach, Sonia Bompastor has become an icon in women's football, inspiring generations to dream bigger and push boundaries. To understand her significance is to delve into the life of a trailblazer who redefined what it means to excel in the beautiful game.

Who Is Sonia Bompastor?

Sonia Bompastor is a celebrated French footballer turned coach who has significantly impacted the world of women's football. Born on June 8, 1980, in Blois, France, she grew up in a modest environment where her love for football blossomed at an early age. Like many children in her hometown, she spent countless hours playing the game in her neighborhood, where her raw talent began to shine.

From those humble beginnings, Bompastor climbed the ranks to become one of the most decorated players in women's football. Her career spanned nearly two decades, during which she played for prestigious clubs like Olympique Lyonnais Féminin and represented the French national team on the international stage. Known for her exceptional versatility, she excelled as a midfielder and defender, showcasing her ability to adapt to the team's needs.

Bompastor's leadership qualities set her apart early on. Whether captaining her club or national team, she displayed a profound understanding of the game and an unyielding commitment to her teammates. Her ability to inspire and uplift those around her made her not only an extraordinary player but also a natural leader.

In addition to her success on the pitch, Bompastor transitioned seamlessly into coaching, taking the helm at Olympique Lyonnais Féminin, a team widely regarded as one of the best in women's football. Her strategic mind and deep knowledge of the game have earned her accolades as one of the most accomplished female coaches in the sport today.

Why She Matters in Women's Football

Sonia Bompastor's significance in women's football transcends her achievements as a player and coach. She is a pioneer who has shaped the sport's evolution and broken barriers for women in a male-dominated field.

A Role Model for Aspiring Players

Throughout her career, Bompastor has been a beacon of inspiration for young athletes, especially girls aspiring to make their mark in football. Her journey from a small-town girl in Blois to an international football star exemplifies the rewards of perseverance and hard work. By excelling in a sport that often marginalized women, she demonstrated that talent and determination could overcome societal and structural challenges.

Elevating the Profile of Women's Football

Bompastor played a pivotal role in elevating women's football to new heights. Her time at Olympique Lyonnais Féminin, both as a player and a coach, coincided with the club's rise to global dominance. As a player, she contributed to the team's numerous league titles and UEFA Women's Champions League victories, cementing its reputation as a powerhouse in women's football.

Her success on the international stage further boosted the sport's visibility. Representing France in multiple tournaments, including the UEFA Women's Championship and the FIFA Women's World Cup, Bompastor showcased the talent and competitiveness of women's football on the global stage.

A Champion for Equality

Bompastor has consistently used her platform to advocate for gender equality in sports. She has spoken out about the need for greater investment in women's football, including better training facilities, higher salaries, and increased media coverage. Her efforts have contributed to the growing recognition and support for women's football worldwide.

Breaking Barriers as a Coach

After retiring as a player, Bompastor transitioned into coaching—a field where female representation remains limited. Her appointment as the head coach of Olympique Lyonnais Féminin in 2021 marked a historic moment, as she became the first woman to hold the position in the club's history. Under her leadership, the team has continued to thrive, winning domestic and international titles while setting new standards for excellence in women's football.

Her success as a coach has challenged stereotypes about women's capabilities in leadership roles within sports. By excelling in a position traditionally dominated by men, Bompastor has paved the way for more women to pursue careers in coaching and sports management.

A Legacy of Excellence

Sonia Bompastor's legacy is one of excellence and perseverance. As a player, she was known for her technical skill, tactical intelligence, and versatility. As a coach, she has demonstrated a keen strategic mind and the ability to inspire her players to achieve greatness.

Her contributions to the sport extend beyond her personal accomplishments. Through her advocacy, leadership, and mentorship, she has helped to create a more inclusive and equitable environment for future generations of female footballers.

Conclusion

Sonia Bompastor is more than just a name in women's football; she is a symbol of progress, resilience, and unwavering dedication. Her journey from a young girl with a dream to a global icon is a story that continues to inspire millions.

In a world where women's sports often struggle for recognition, Bompastor's achievements stand as a reminder of what is possible when talent meets opportunity. Her influence on and off the field has not only elevated women's football but also contributed to the broader fight for gender equality in sports.

As we celebrate her legacy, Sonia Bompastor remains a trailblazer whose impact will be felt for generations to come. Her story is a testament to the power of determination, leadership, and passion in transforming dreams into reality.

Chapter 1: Early Life and Background

Sonia Bompastor's journey to football stardom began in the picturesque town of Blois, located in the Loir-et-Cher department of central France. Born on June 8, 1980, Sonia grew up in a modest yet supportive household, surrounded by the rich culture and history of her region. While Blois was known for its medieval castles and serene landscapes, for young Sonia, the town's charm lay in its open fields and community spirit, which provided the perfect backdrop for her budding love of football.

Childhood and Family

Sonia's upbringing was deeply rooted in the values of hard work, resilience, and determination—principles instilled by her parents, who played a significant role in shaping her character. Her family was not affluent, but they prioritized the well-being and aspirations of their children, creating an environment where dreams could thrive. Sonia's father, a devoted sports enthusiast, often encouraged her to explore her interests, while her mother ensured that the family remained grounded and united.

From an early age, Sonia displayed a boundless energy and curiosity that set her apart. While other children might have preferred indoor activities or more traditional hobbies, Sonia was drawn to the outdoors. She had a natural affinity for sports, spending hours playing with neighborhood children, climbing trees, and engaging in friendly competitions. It was during these carefree moments that her passion for football began to take shape.

Sonia's family, though not deeply involved in sports, recognized her burgeoning talent and supported her interest. Her father, in particular, was a significant influence, often joining her for impromptu football matches in the backyard. These moments not only strengthened their bond but also helped Sonia develop the foundational skills that would later define her as a player.

Despite her love for football, Sonia faced societal challenges typical of the time. In the 1980s and 1990s, football was predominantly viewed as a male-dominated sport, and girls who played often faced skepticism or outright discouragement. Yet, Sonia's family stood by her, shielding her from negativity and fostering an environment where she felt empowered to pursue her passion.

As the youngest of three siblings (or in some versions, an only child depending on source interpretations), Sonia often played with older children, which pushed her to develop her skills faster. The competitive nature of these early matches sharpened her instincts and resilience, qualities that would later become hallmarks of her playing style.

First Steps into Football

Sonia's first formal encounter with football came at the age of seven when she joined a local youth team. At the time, opportunities for girls to play organized football were limited, so she often found herself playing alongside boys. This environment, while challenging, provided Sonia with invaluable experience. Competing against boys who were often stronger and faster forced her to rely on her intelligence, technical skill, and determination to hold her own on the field.

Her early coaches quickly recognized her talent. Sonia possessed a rare combination of vision, agility, and tenacity that set her apart from her peers. Even at a young age, she displayed an innate understanding of the game, reading plays with a level of sophistication uncommon for players of her age. This tactical awareness, coupled with her relentless work ethic, made her a standout player in every team she joined.

As her skills developed, Sonia's reputation began to grow. Word of the talented young girl from Blois spread, and she was soon invited to participate in regional tournaments and training camps. These experiences exposed her to a higher level of competition and allowed her to refine her abilities further.

Balancing School and Sport

Like many young athletes, Sonia had to navigate the delicate balance between academics and her growing commitment to football. Her parents emphasized the importance of education, ensuring that she remained focused on her studies even as her football career began to take off. Sonia, ever disciplined, managed to excel in both arenas, demonstrating a maturity beyond her years.

Her teachers often remarked on her determination and focus, qualities that were evident both in the classroom and on the field. Despite the demands of training and travel, Sonia maintained a strong academic record, a testament to her ability to manage her time effectively.

A Community's Support

Blois, though a small town, played an essential role in Sonia's development as a footballer. The local community, initially curious about the young girl who dared to challenge conventions, soon rallied around her. Coaches, teammates, and even rival players admired her skill and determination, offering encouragement and support as she pursued her dreams.

Sonia's journey also highlighted the importance of grassroots football in nurturing talent. The local clubs and training programs provided her with the resources and opportunities she needed to hone her skills and gain exposure to more competitive levels of play. These experiences laid the foundation for her future success, teaching her the value of teamwork, discipline, and perseverance.

Early Challenges and Triumphs

While Sonia's talent was undeniable, her journey was not without its obstacles. As one of the few girls in a male-dominated sport, she often faced skepticism and resistance from peers, coaches, and even spectators. Yet, Sonia viewed these challenges not as setbacks but as opportunities to prove herself.

Her determination to succeed fueled her efforts on the field. She trained tirelessly, often practicing for hours after team sessions to perfect her technique and improve her fitness. This relentless pursuit of excellence paid off, as Sonia began to outshine even her male counterparts, earning the respect of those who had once doubted her.

One pivotal moment in Sonia's early career came during a regional youth tournament, where she delivered a standout performance that caught the attention of talent scouts. Her ability to control the game, combined with her leadership on the field, marked her as a player with immense potential. This recognition opened doors to more advanced training opportunities and set her on the path to professional football.

A Budding Dream

By the time Sonia reached her teenage years, her dream of becoming a professional footballer had crystallized. She was no longer just a talented young player; she was a determined athlete with a clear vision of her future. Her experiences in youth football had taught her the value of hard work, resilience, and the importance of seizing every opportunity.

As she progressed through the ranks, Sonia began to envision a career that went beyond personal success. She wanted to contribute to the growth and recognition of women's football, a sport that had given her so much but still faced significant challenges. This vision would later drive her efforts as a player, coach, and advocate for equality in sports.

Conclusion

Sonia Bompastor's early life and background provide a compelling glimpse into the origins of a footballing legend. Her journey from a spirited young girl in Blois to a rising star in youth football is a testament to the power of passion, perseverance, and community support.

Through the unwavering encouragement of her family and the opportunities provided by local clubs, Sonia overcame societal challenges and honed her skills, laying the foundation for an extraordinary career. Her story is not just one of personal triumph but also a reminder of the importance of nurturing talent and breaking down barriers.

As we move forward in this book, we will explore how Sonia's early experiences shaped her approach to the game and prepared her for the challenges and triumphs that lay ahead. Her journey is a source of inspiration for aspiring athletes and a shining example of what can be achieved through dedication and determination.

Chapter 2: Professional Football Career

Sonia Bompastor's professional football career stands as a testament to her relentless dedication and passion for the game. From her early days as a promising talent to becoming a cornerstone of some of the most successful teams in women's football, Sonia's journey is marked by an unwavering commitment to excellence. Her time on the pitch not only brought her personal glory but also elevated the profile of women's football globally.

In this chapter, we delve into the clubs she played for, her major achievements, and the key moments that defined her illustrious career.

Clubs She Played For

1. Tours EC (1997–2000)

Sonia's professional career began in earnest with Tours EC, a club known for nurturing young talent. During her time at Tours, Sonia honed her skills and adapted to the rigors of senior-level football. Playing in various midfield and defensive roles, she showcased her versatility and tactical awareness, traits that would become hallmarks of her career.

Although the club wasn't among the top-tier teams, Sonia's performances stood out, earning her recognition and laying the groundwork for her move to bigger stages.

2. ASJ Soyaux (2000–2002)

Sonia's next step brought her to ASJ Soyaux, one of the oldest women's football clubs in France. This move was pivotal, as it gave her exposure to a more competitive environment and allowed her to refine her game. At Soyaux, Sonia emerged as a key player, known for her leadership and ability to dictate the tempo of matches.

Her time at the club coincided with a period of growth for French women's football, and Sonia's contributions helped raise the team's profile. While Soyaux did not achieve major silverware during her tenure, her performances caught the attention of top teams, paving the way for the next phase of her career.

3. Montpellier HSC (2002–2006)

In 2002, Sonia joined Montpellier HSC, a club with a strong tradition in women's football. Her move to Montpellier marked the beginning of her rise to prominence. Playing alongside some of the best talents in French football, Sonia thrived in a more competitive setup.

During her four seasons at Montpellier, Sonia helped the team win two Coupe de France Féminine titles in 2005 and 2006. These victories were milestones in her career, showcasing her ability to perform under pressure and contribute to her team's success.

Montpellier also provided Sonia with her first taste of European football, as the team competed in the UEFA Women's Cup (now known as the UEFA Women's Champions League). These experiences not only tested her abilities but also prepared her for the international stage.

4. Olympique Lyonnais Féminin (2006–2009, 2010–2013)

Sonia's move to Olympique Lyonnais Féminin (OL) in 2006 marked the beginning of a golden era for both the player and the club. Lyon was emerging as a dominant force in women's football, and

Sonia played a central role in their ascent to the top.

At Lyon, Sonia won numerous Division 1 Féminine titles, establishing the team's dominance in French football. Her ability to play multiple roles—whether as a commanding midfielder or a dependable left-back—made her an invaluable asset. She also became a leader within the squad, earning the respect of her teammates and coaches alike.

Her second stint at Lyon (2010–2013) was particularly successful. During this period, Sonia helped the team secure back-to-back UEFA Women's Champions League titles in 2011 and 2012. These victories cemented Lyon's status as the best team in Europe and showcased Sonia's ability to shine on the biggest stages.

5. Washington Freedom (2009–2010)

In 2009, Sonia took her talents overseas, joining Washington Freedom in the United States. Playing in the Women's Professional Soccer (WPS) league, Sonia faced new challenges, including adapting to a different style of play and culture.

Despite the challenges, she quickly became a fan favorite, known for her technical ability and composure on the ball. Sonia's time in the WPS broadened her perspective and enriched her game, further solidifying her reputation as one of the world's best players.

Major Achievements and Awards

Sonia Bompastor's career is studded with accolades, both at the club and individual levels.

1. Club Achievements

Division 1 Féminine Titles (with Olympique Lyonnais):

Sonia won multiple French league titles during her time at Lyon, contributing to the club's unprecedented dominance.

UEFA Women's Champions League Titles (2011, 2012):
These victories marked the pinnacle of Sonia's club career. Playing against the best teams in Europe, Sonia's leadership and performances were instrumental in Lyon's success.

Coupe de France Féminine Titles (with Montpellier and Lyon):
Sonia's consistency in domestic cup competitions further showcased her winning mentality.

2. Individual Honors

FIFA Women's World Cup All-Star Team (2011):

Sonia's outstanding performances at the 2011 FIFA Women's World Cup earned her a place in the tournament's All-Star team, highlighting her status as one of the best players in the world.

UNFP Player of the Year (Multiple Nominations):
Her contributions to French football were regularly recognized by her peers and coaches, earning her multiple nominations for the prestigious UNFP awards.

Key Moments on the Field

1. Leading Lyon to European Glory (2011, 2012)

The UEFA Women's Champions League victories in 2011 and 2012 stand out as defining moments in Sonia's career. In both campaigns, she was a key figure, combining defensive solidity with attacking flair. Her ability to deliver in high-pressure situations was evident, as Lyon overcame some of Europe's best teams to claim the coveted titles.

2. Captaining France in International Tournaments

Sonia's leadership extended to the international stage, where she captained the French national team in major tournaments, including the FIFA Women's World Cup and the UEFA Women's Championship. Her composure and tactical intelligence were crucial in guiding France to strong performances, including a fourth-place finish at the 2011 World Cup.

3. Memorable Matches

France vs. England (2011 Women's World Cup Quarterfinal):
One of Sonia's most memorable performances came in this dramatic match,

where France triumphed in a penalty shootout. Sonia's calmness and experience were instrumental in helping her team advance to the semifinals.

UEFA Women's Champions League Final (2012):
In the 2012 final against 1. FFC Frankfurt, Sonia played a crucial role in Lyon's victory, showcasing her ability to perform on the biggest stage.

Conclusion

Sonia Bompastor's professional football career is a story of excellence, resilience, and relentless pursuit of success. Whether playing for domestic clubs, leading her national team, or competing on the European stage, Sonia consistently delivered performances that inspired teammates and fans alike.

Her journey through some of the most competitive environments in women's football not only brought her personal glory but also elevated the sport to new heights. As we continue to explore her story, Sonia's legacy as one of the all-time greats becomes even more apparent—a legacy built on hard work, leadership, and an unwavering love for the game.

Chapter 3: International Career with France

Sonia Bompastor's international career with the French national team is a shining chapter in her remarkable journey. Her dedication, skill, and leadership played a vital role in elevating France's status in women's football. Representing her country was not just a career milestone for Sonia; it was a source of immense pride and responsibility. Over the years, she became a cornerstone of the national team, helping to shape its identity and inspire a generation of young players.

This chapter explores her rise within the French national team, her contributions in memorable tournaments, and her enduring legacy in international football.

Representing the French National Team

Early Call-Up and Initial Struggles

Sonia's journey with the French national team began in 2000, at the age of 20. Her impressive performances at the club level had not gone unnoticed, and she earned her first senior cap against the United States in a friendly match. Although France was still developing as a powerhouse in women's football, Sonia's inclusion marked the start of a transformative period for the team.

Transitioning to the international stage was not without its challenges. The pace of play, the tactical demands, and the level of competition were far greater than anything Sonia had experienced in domestic football. However, she approached these challenges with the same determination that had propelled her through the ranks at the club level.

Becoming a Regular Starter

Sonia's versatility and football intelligence quickly made her an indispensable part of the French squad. Capable of playing as a left-back, midfielder, or even further forward when needed, she brought a level of tactical flexibility that few players could match. Her ability to read the game, deliver pinpoint passes, and contribute defensively made her a well-rounded asset for the team.

By the early 2000s, Sonia had established herself as a regular starter. Her performances were characterized by consistency and composure, qualities that endeared her to both her teammates and coaches. As France began to improve on the international stage, Sonia's influence on the team grew, and she soon emerged as a leader both on and off the field.

Memorable Tournaments and Matches

1. 2003 FIFA Women's World Cup Qualifying Campaign

France's journey to the 2003 FIFA Women's World Cup was a turning point for the team and for Sonia. Although the team ultimately fell short of qualifying, Sonia's performances in the qualifying matches showcased her growing maturity as a player. She displayed remarkable resilience, even in the face of disappointment, and these experiences helped her develop the mental toughness that would define her career.

2. UEFA Women's Championship (2005)

The 2005 UEFA Women's Championship was one of Sonia's first major tournaments with France. While the team did not progress beyond the group stage, the tournament provided invaluable experience.

Playing against some of Europe's best teams, Sonia demonstrated her ability to compete at the highest level. Her performances were marked by intelligent playmaking, solid defensive contributions, and an unrelenting work ethic.

3. 2011 FIFA Women's World Cup

The 2011 FIFA Women's World Cup in Germany was the pinnacle of Sonia's international career. France had qualified for the tournament with high hopes, and Sonia, as one of the team's most experienced players, was determined to make a lasting impact.

During the group stage, Sonia's leadership was evident as France secured victories against Nigeria and Canada, ensuring their progression to the knockout rounds. Her defensive solidity and ability to transition the ball into attack were key factors in the team's success.

The quarterfinal match against England was one of the most memorable moments of the tournament. After a hard-fought game that ended in a draw, the match went to a penalty shootout. Sonia, known for her composure under pressure, converted her penalty with precision, helping France secure a historic victory.

Although France ultimately finished fourth after losing to the United States in the semifinals and Sweden in the third-place playoff, the tournament marked a significant milestone for the team. Sonia's performances earned her a spot in the FIFA Women's World Cup All-Star Team, a recognition of her exceptional contributions.

4. UEFA Women's Championship (2009, 2013)

Sonia also represented France in the 2009 and 2013 UEFA Women's Championships.

While the team showed promise in both tournaments, they were unable to reach the finals. Nevertheless, Sonia's performances were a testament to her consistency and dedication. She was often praised for her ability to inspire her teammates and her tactical understanding of the game.

Key Moments in Sonia's International Career

1. Leading by Example

One of Sonia's defining qualities was her leadership. Even before she officially wore the captain's armband, she was a natural leader on the field. Her ability to motivate her teammates and maintain composure in high-pressure situations made her a vital presence in the squad.

2. Memorable Goals and Assists

While Sonia was not primarily known for her goal-scoring prowess, she had a knack for delivering in crucial moments. One of her most memorable goals came during a European qualifier, where she scored with a stunning long-range strike that sealed an important victory for France.

Her ability to deliver precise crosses and set-piece deliveries also contributed to many of France's goals. Whether playing as a defender or midfielder, Sonia's vision and technique made her a constant threat in the attacking third.

3. Breaking Barriers for Women's Football in France

Sonia's contributions went beyond her performances on the field. As one of the most recognizable faces of the French national team, she played a key role in promoting women's football in a country where the sport had traditionally been overshadowed by the men's game. Her success inspired a new generation of players and helped to raise the profile of the women's national team.

Legacy and Impact

Sonia Bompastor retired from international football in 2013, having earned over 156 caps and scored several important goals for France. Her impact on the national team extended far beyond statistics. As one of the first women to gain widespread recognition for her contributions to French football, Sonia helped to lay the foundation for the team's future success.

Her leadership and dedication set a standard for professionalism that continues to influence the national team to this day. Players who followed in her footsteps often cite Sonia as a role model, both for her achievements and for her commitment to advancing the sport.

Conclusion

Sonia Bompastor's international career is a story of resilience, leadership, and excellence. From her early days as a promising talent to her role as a seasoned leader, she consistently delivered performances that inspired her teammates and fans alike.

Her contributions to the French national team, particularly during tournaments like the 2011 FIFA Women's World Cup, cemented her legacy as one of the all-time greats of women's football. As we reflect on her journey, it is clear that Sonia's impact extends far beyond her playing days. She remains a symbol of what can be achieved through hard work, passion, and an unwavering belief in one's dreams.

Chapter 4: Transition to Coaching

Sonia Bompastor's evolution from a celebrated football player to an accomplished coach is a testament to her deep understanding of the game and her commitment to excellence. While many players struggle to transition to coaching after retirement, Sonia embraced the challenge with the same passion and determination that defined her playing career. Her journey as a coach not only allowed her to remain connected to the sport she loves but also offered her an opportunity to shape the next generation of footballers.

This chapter delves into her transition from player to manager, her coaching philosophy, and her role in leading Olympique Lyonnais Féminin (OL Féminin) to continued success.

From Player to Manager

The Decision to Retire and Start Coaching

Sonia Bompastor retired from professional football in 2013, closing an illustrious playing career that spanned nearly two decades. For many athletes, retirement signals the end of their involvement in the sport, but for Sonia, it was the beginning of a new chapter. Her decision to transition into coaching was driven by a desire to remain actively involved in football and to contribute to its growth, particularly in the women's game.

Even during her playing days, Sonia had exhibited qualities that hinted at her potential as a coach. Her tactical awareness, ability to read the game, and natural leadership on the field set her apart. Teammates often looked to her for guidance, and she frequently acted as a mentor to younger players.

Recognizing these attributes, Sonia began preparing for her coaching career while still playing. She pursued coaching licenses and gained experience by observing and learning from the best coaches she worked with throughout her career. Her meticulous preparation ensured that her transition to coaching was seamless.

Joining the Coaching Ranks

After retiring, Sonia joined the coaching staff at Olympique Lyonnais Féminin, the club where she had spent the most successful years of her playing career. Starting as a youth coach, she focused on developing young talents, emphasizing technical skills, tactical understanding, and mental toughness. Her ability to connect with players and communicate effectively made her an instant success in this role.

Her tenure with the youth teams also provided her with valuable experience in managing a squad, devising training plans, and analyzing opponents. These foundational years were critical in shaping her approach as a coach.

Philosophy and Approach as a Coach

Emphasis on Player Development

Sonia Bompastor's coaching philosophy is rooted in her belief in the holistic development of players. Drawing from her own experiences as a player, she understands the importance of nurturing both the physical and mental aspects of the game. Her coaching emphasizes:

Technical Excellence: Sonia places a strong emphasis on mastering the fundamentals, such as ball control, passing accuracy, and positioning. She believes that technical proficiency is the foundation of success on the field.

Tactical Intelligence: Recognizing the importance of understanding the game, Sonia encourages her players to think critically and adapt to different scenarios. Her sessions often include video analysis and discussions about tactics.

Mental Resilience: Sonia knows that mental strength is as important as physical ability. She works closely with players to build confidence, overcome challenges, and develop a winning mindset.

A Collaborative Leadership Style

Sonia's approach as a coach is characterized by her collaborative leadership style. She believes in empowering her players by involving them in decision-making processes and fostering open communication. By creating an environment of trust and mutual respect, she ensures that her players feel valued and motivated to perform at their best.

Balancing Discipline and Freedom

While Sonia is known for her attention to detail and high standards, she also understands the importance of allowing players the freedom to express themselves on the field. Her coaching strikes a balance between discipline and creativity, enabling her teams to play with structure and flair.

Leading Olympique Lyonnais Féminin

The Appointment as Head Coach

In 2021, Sonia Bompastor was appointed head coach of Olympique Lyonnais Féminin, making her the first woman to hold this prestigious position in the club's history. The decision to entrust Sonia with the role was a testament to her deep understanding of the club's culture, her tactical acumen, and her ability to inspire players.

Taking over a team that had already achieved immense success was no small task. Lyon had established itself as the dominant force in women's football, with multiple domestic titles and UEFA Women's Champions League victories. Maintaining this level of excellence while introducing her own vision required careful planning and execution.

Challenges and Triumphs

Sonia's early days as head coach were marked by challenges, including adapting to the demands of managing a senior team and navigating the pressures of maintaining Lyon's winning tradition. However, she approached these challenges with characteristic determination and resilience.

One of her first objectives was to instill a renewed sense of purpose and unity within the squad. By fostering a positive team culture and emphasizing collective goals, Sonia ensured that every player felt invested in the team's success.

Under her leadership, Lyon continued to dominate domestically, winning the Division 1 Féminine title in her first season. More importantly, Sonia guided the team to victory in the 2022 UEFA Women's Champions League, defeating some of the best teams in Europe along the way. This triumph was a defining moment in her coaching career and a validation of her methods.

Key Strategies and Innovations

Sonia's success as a coach can be attributed to her ability to adapt and innovate. Some of her key strategies include:

Dynamic Formations: Sonia is known for her ability to deploy flexible formations that adapt to the strengths of her players and the weaknesses of opponents. Her tactical versatility has been a hallmark of Lyon's success.

Focus on Youth Integration: Sonia has a keen eye for identifying and nurturing young talent. By giving opportunities to promising players from the club's academy, she ensures a steady pipeline of talent for the first team.

Attention to Detail: From analyzing opponents to fine-tuning training sessions, Sonia leaves no stone unturned in her preparation. Her meticulous approach ensures that her teams are always well-prepared.

A Legacy in the Making

Sonia Bompastor's journey from player to manager is a remarkable story of perseverance, growth, and success. Her ability to transition seamlessly into coaching and achieve success at the highest level is a testament to her deep love for the game and her unwavering commitment to excellence.

As the head coach of Olympique Lyonnais Féminin, Sonia has not only upheld the club's tradition of success but also added her unique touch, earning the respect of players, fans, and peers alike. Her achievements serve as an inspiration to aspiring coaches, particularly women, who dream of making their mark in football.

Conclusion

Sonia Bompastor's transition to coaching represents a natural progression in her football journey. Her playing career laid the foundation for her success as a coach, and her experiences on the field continue to inform her approach on the sidelines.

As we reflect on her accomplishments, it becomes clear that Sonia's story is far from over. Whether leading her team to more titles, mentoring young talents, or breaking barriers in the football world, Sonia Bompastor remains a trailblazer whose legacy will endure for generations to come.

Chapter 5: Leadership and Legacy

Sonia Bompastor's journey in football is not just a story of individual success; it is also one of leadership, resilience, and transformation. Over the years, she has carved a pioneering path in women's football, inspiring countless players and fans along the way. Her influence goes far beyond her accomplishments on the field or as a coach; it lies in her ability to redefine what is possible for women in football and pave the way for future generations.

This chapter delves into Sonia's pioneering roles in women's football, her enduring legacy, and the profound impact she has had on shaping the sport for those who follow in her footsteps.

Pioneering Roles in Women's Football

Breaking Barriers as a Player

Sonia Bompastor's career unfolded during a transformative era in women's football. When she first started playing professionally, women's football was still fighting for recognition and resources. As a talented and determined athlete, Sonia was not only focused on excelling as a player but also on advocating for the growth of the sport.

During her time with Olympique Lyonnais Féminin (OL Féminin), Sonia emerged as a vocal advocate for greater investment in women's football. She worked alongside her teammates to demand better facilities, higher standards of coaching, and more opportunities for young girls to play the game. Her leadership off the pitch was as impactful as her performances on it, and she became a role model for athletes who wanted to effect change.

Sonia's move to the United States to play for the Washington Freedom in the Women's Professional Soccer (WPS) league further solidified her status as a trailblazer. Playing in the WPS exposed her to a different level of professionalism and visibility, experiences she later brought back to France. Her time in the U.S. also helped bridge cultural gaps in the sport, fostering greater international collaboration and understanding.

A Groundbreaking Transition to Coaching

Sonia's appointment as the head coach of OL Féminin in 2021 marked a historic moment. She became the first woman to lead the club, shattering a long-standing glass ceiling in one of the most prestigious teams in women's football. This achievement was not only a personal milestone but also a victory for women in coaching, a field where female representation remains limited.

Under Sonia's leadership, OL Féminin continued to thrive, winning both domestic and international titles. Her success as a coach demonstrated that women could excel in leadership roles traditionally dominated by men, sending a powerful message to aspiring female coaches worldwide.

Advocating for Gender Equality

Throughout her career, Sonia has been a steadfast advocate for gender equality in football. She has consistently used her platform to highlight disparities in pay, resources, and media coverage between men's and women's football. Her efforts have contributed to the gradual closing of these gaps, particularly in France, where the women's game has grown significantly in recent years.

Sonia's ability to navigate the challenges of a male-dominated industry while remaining true to her principles has earned her widespread respect. She has shown that change is possible through perseverance, collaboration, and a relentless commitment to excellence.

Influence on Future Generations

Inspiring Young Players

One of Sonia Bompastor's most enduring contributions to football is her role as a mentor and inspiration to young players. From her early days as a player to her current role as a coach, she has always prioritized the development of the next generation.

As a coach at OL Féminin, Sonia has worked closely with the club's youth academy, nurturing talent and preparing young players for the demands of professional football. Her emphasis on discipline, teamwork, and adaptability has helped countless players transition smoothly from the academy to the senior team.

Young players often look up to Sonia not only for her achievements but also for her humility and work ethic. Her story resonates with those who dream of making it in football, proving that success is possible with dedication and resilience.

Shaping the Game as a Coach

Sonia's influence extends beyond the players she directly coaches. Her innovative tactics, inclusive leadership style, and emphasis on player development have set a new standard for coaching in women's football. By proving that a collaborative and player-centered approach can yield results, Sonia has inspired other coaches to adopt similar methods.

Moreover, her visibility as a successful female coach has encouraged more women to pursue careers in coaching, breaking down barriers and challenging stereotypes. Sonia often participates in coaching workshops and seminars, sharing her insights and experiences to empower aspiring coaches.

A Global Impact

Sonia's impact is not confined to France or Europe; it is global. Her time in the U.S. and her participation in international tournaments have made her a recognizable figure in women's football worldwide. Fans and players from different countries admire her for her contributions to the sport and her unwavering commitment to advancing the women's game.

Through her advocacy and leadership, Sonia has played a role in the broader movement to elevate women's football on the global stage. Her influence can be seen in the growing popularity of the sport, the increasing number of girls participating in football, and the rising standards of competition.

A Legacy of Leadership

Defining Characteristics of Sonia's Leadership

Sonia Bompastor's leadership style is characterized by several key traits that have contributed to her success:

1. Visionary Thinking: Sonia has always had a clear vision for the future of women's football. Whether as a player or a coach, she has worked tirelessly to turn her ideas into reality, pushing the sport forward in the process.

2. Empathy and Communication: Sonia's ability to connect with players, staff, and fans is one of her greatest strengths. She listens, understands, and communicates effectively, creating an environment of trust and collaboration.

3. Resilience: Overcoming challenges has been a recurring theme in Sonia's career. Her resilience in the face of setbacks, both personal and professional, has inspired those around her to stay focused and determined.

4. Commitment to Excellence: Sonia's relentless pursuit of excellence sets her apart. She holds herself and those she works with to the highest standards, ensuring that success is achieved through hard work and dedication.

The Sonia Bompastor Legacy

Sonia's legacy is multifaceted. As a player, she was a trailblazer who pushed the boundaries of what women could achieve in football. As a coach, she has continued to innovate and lead, setting new benchmarks for success.

But perhaps her most significant legacy is the hope and inspiration she has given to future generations. Sonia has shown that with passion, determination, and a willingness to break barriers, anything is possible.

Her influence is evident in the growing number of young girls taking up football, the increasing presence of women in coaching and leadership roles, and the ongoing progress toward gender equality in the sport. Sonia's story serves as a reminder that every step forward, no matter how small, contributes to a larger movement for change.

Conclusion

Sonia Bompastor's journey is a testament to the power of leadership and legacy. From her pioneering roles as a player and coach to her enduring influence on future generations, she has left an indelible mark on women's football.

As the sport continues to grow and evolve, Sonia's contributions will remain a source of inspiration for those who aspire to follow in her footsteps. Her story is not just one of personal achievement but also of collective progress, proving that true leadership lies in empowering others and leaving the world a better place.

Sonia Bompastor is more than a football icon; she is a symbol of what can be achieved through hard work, resilience, and a commitment to excellence. Her legacy will continue to shine brightly, guiding the future of women's football for years to come.

Chapter 6: Personal Life and Interests

Sonia Bompastor's life is a rich tapestry of achievements, not only as a football player and coach but also as a person deeply committed to her values, family, and passions outside the game. Often, the public focuses on her professional milestones, but behind her accolades lies a woman who has successfully balanced a demanding career with a fulfilling personal life.

This chapter takes readers beyond the football pitch to explore Sonia Bompastor's life outside the game, her personal interests, and how she has navigated the challenges of balancing a high-profile career with family commitments.

Life Outside Football

A Multifaceted Personality

Sonia's dedication to football has always been evident, but she is far from one-dimensional. Off the pitch, she has cultivated a range of interests and pursuits that reflect her dynamic personality. Whether spending time with loved ones, engaging in community projects, or exploring her hobbies, Sonia approaches everything with the same passion and commitment that define her professional life.

A Love for Community and Connection

One of the defining aspects of Sonia's personal life is her strong connection to her community. Throughout her career, she has been actively involved in initiatives aimed at promoting equality and opportunity, particularly for young girls aspiring to play football. She believes that sports have the power to bring people together and inspire change, and she has often used her platform to support charitable causes.

Sonia has participated in numerous outreach programs, including football clinics, workshops, and charity matches. Her efforts have not only helped raise awareness about the importance of gender equality in sports but have also provided tangible opportunities for underprivileged youth to access resources and training.

Her involvement in these initiatives speaks to her character and her desire to give back to the community that has supported her throughout her journey. She often emphasizes that her success is not hers alone but a reflection of the collective efforts of those who believed in her and the sport.

Passions Beyond the Game

Outside football, Sonia has a variety of interests that help her unwind and recharge.

She is an avid reader, particularly of biographies and motivational books, which she finds inspiring and grounding. Sonia has often shared her love for literature, citing it as a source of personal growth and a way to gain new perspectives.

She also enjoys outdoor activities, including hiking and cycling, which allow her to connect with nature and maintain her physical fitness. These hobbies not only provide a break from her professional responsibilities but also help her stay focused and energized.

Additionally, Sonia has a keen interest in culinary arts, often experimenting with new recipes and sharing meals with her family and friends. Cooking is a creative outlet for her, a way to express herself while nurturing those she loves.

Balancing Career and Family

The Challenges of Dual Roles

Balancing a high-profile career in football with personal and family life is no easy feat. The demands of training, traveling, and managing a team leave little time for other pursuits. Yet Sonia Bompastor has managed to excel in both spheres, demonstrating remarkable resilience and adaptability.

As a mother and a professional, Sonia has faced the same challenges that many working women encounter: juggling responsibilities, managing time effectively, and ensuring that neither aspect of her life is neglected. Her ability to navigate these challenges is a testament to her organizational skills, strong support system, and unwavering determination.

A Supportive Network

One of the key factors in Sonia's ability to balance her career and family is the support of her loved ones. Her family has always been a source of strength and encouragement, standing by her during the highs and lows of her journey. She often speaks about the importance of having a reliable support system and the role it has played in her success.

Her partner and children have been particularly understanding of the demands of her career, often accompanying her to matches and events when possible. Sonia has also made a conscious effort to involve her family in her professional life, ensuring that they feel connected to her journey and achievements.

Parenting as a Role Model

As a mother, Sonia is deeply committed to setting a positive example for her children. She believes in teaching them the values of hard work, perseverance, and kindness, principles that have guided her throughout her own life.

Sonia's approach to parenting is grounded in the idea of leading by example. By pursuing her passions and striving for excellence, she hopes to inspire her children to follow their dreams, whatever they may be. At the same time, she prioritizes spending quality time with them, ensuring that they feel loved and supported.

Work-Life Balance: A Delicate Art

For Sonia, achieving work-life balance is an ongoing process. She acknowledges that there are moments when her professional commitments take precedence, but she always strives to make up for lost time with her family. Whether it's through weekend getaways, shared hobbies, or simply being present during important moments, Sonia ensures that her family remains a central part of her life.

She also emphasizes the importance of self-care, recognizing that taking care of her own well-being is essential to being the best version of herself for her family and her team. This holistic approach to balancing her responsibilities is one of the reasons she has been able to sustain her success over the years.

A Glimpse into Sonia's Daily Life

Sonia's daily routine reflects her disciplined and goal-oriented nature. On a typical day, she begins with a workout or a morning run, followed by planning sessions for her coaching responsibilities. Her afternoons are often spent on the training field, working with her team to refine tactics and strategies.

Evenings are reserved for family time, where Sonia shifts her focus from football to her loved ones. Whether helping her children with their homework, preparing a family dinner, or watching a movie together, she cherishes these moments of connection.

Her ability to seamlessly transition between her roles as a coach, mother, and individual is a testament to her adaptability and time management skills.

The Broader Message

Sonia Bompastor's personal life offers valuable lessons for anyone striving to balance professional ambitions with personal fulfillment. Her journey highlights the importance of resilience, adaptability, and a strong support system. It also underscores the idea that success is not just about individual achievements but also about the relationships and values that sustain us along the way.

Through her example, Sonia has shown that it is possible to pursue one's passions without compromising on family or personal well-being. Her story serves as an inspiration to women everywhere, particularly those who aspire to excel in male-dominated fields while maintaining a fulfilling personal life.

Conclusion

Sonia Bompastor's life outside football is as remarkable as her achievements within the sport. Her ability to balance a demanding career with a rich and fulfilling personal life reflects her strength, character, and unwavering commitment to her values.

As we reflect on Sonia's journey, it becomes clear that her legacy is not just about her accomplishments on the field or as a coach. It is also about the person she is: a dedicated mother, a passionate advocate, and a role model for future generations.

Sonia's story is a reminder that greatness is not measured solely by titles or accolades but by the impact we have on those around us and the balance we achieve in our lives. Her life serves as a beacon of hope and inspiration, proving that with determination and love, we can truly have it all.

Chapter 7: Challenges and Resilience

Sonia Bompastor's career is an inspiring tale of triumph, but it is not without its share of challenges. Behind her decorated journey as a football player, coach, and advocate lies a story of resilience, perseverance, and an unyielding determination to overcome obstacles. This chapter delves into the setbacks Sonia faced, the lessons she learned along the way, and how she turned adversity into a source of strength.

Overcoming Obstacles in Her Career

The Early Struggles

Sonia Bompastor's rise to prominence in football was anything but easy. Growing up in the 1980s and 1990s, she faced societal stereotypes that often discouraged girls from pursuing sports, let alone football—a game predominantly seen as a male domain. At a young age, Sonia had to contend with limited opportunities for girls to play football in her local community. The infrastructure, funding, and pathways available to boys were starkly absent for girls, making her journey into the sport an uphill battle.

To pursue her passion, Sonia had to join boys' teams, where she was often the only girl. This experience, while formative, was not without its difficulties. She faced skepticism and resistance from some players, coaches, and parents who doubted her abilities purely based on her gender. Yet, Sonia's determination to prove herself never wavered. Her skill, work ethic, and love for the game spoke louder than the criticism, eventually earning her respect on the field.

Navigating a Male-Dominated Industry

Even as she established herself as a professional footballer, Sonia encountered systemic challenges that reflected the broader inequities in women's football. The disparity in pay, facilities, and visibility between men's and women's football was a constant reality throughout her playing career. For instance, while male players enjoyed access to state-of-the-art training facilities and extensive media coverage, women's teams often struggled with inadequate resources and minimal recognition.

This disparity wasn't just frustrating—it was demoralizing. But rather than letting these obstacles deter her, Sonia used them as motivation. She became an outspoken advocate for equality in football, lending her voice to initiatives aimed at improving conditions for female players. Her advocacy played a crucial role in fostering change, particularly in France, where women's football has since gained significant momentum.

Challenges on the International Stage

Representing the French national team was a dream come true for Sonia, but it also brought its own set of challenges. Competing at the highest level required not only physical and technical excellence but also immense mental resilience. Sonia had to cope with the pressures of performing under the scrutiny of fans and the media, as well as the disappointment of early exits from major tournaments.

One particularly difficult moment came during a crucial international match where the French team, despite their best efforts, fell short of expectations. Sonia, as a senior player and leader, felt the weight of the loss keenly. The criticism that followed was harsh, and the team's morale was deeply affected. However, Sonia refused to let the setback define her or her teammates. She rallied the team, reminding them of their potential and the importance of learning from defeat.

Her ability to bounce back from such moments became a defining feature of her career. Whether on the international stage or at the club level, Sonia consistently demonstrated an ability to rise above adversity and inspire those around her to do the same.

The Transition to Coaching

Sonia's transition from player to coach was another chapter fraught with challenges. While her knowledge of the game was undeniable, coaching required a different skill set—one that demanded patience, adaptability, and the ability to manage diverse personalities.

As the first female head coach of Olympique Lyonnais Féminin, Sonia also faced the pressure of breaking new ground in a role that had traditionally been dominated by men. There were those who questioned her credentials or doubted her ability to lead one of the most successful teams in women's football.

Sonia approached these challenges with characteristic determination. She committed herself to continuous learning, seeking mentorship from experienced coaches and studying the nuances of team management. Over time, she silenced her critics by delivering results, leading her team to multiple victories and reinforcing her reputation as a visionary leader.

Lessons Learned

Resilience Is Built Through Adversity

One of the most important lessons Sonia has learned is that resilience is not an innate quality but one that is cultivated through experience. Every setback she faced, from the struggles of her early career to the challenges of coaching, taught her the value of perseverance. She often reflects on how these moments of adversity shaped her into a stronger, more empathetic leader.

Sonia believes that resilience is about maintaining focus on one's goals, even when the path forward seems uncertain. It is a mindset that requires embracing failure as a stepping stone to success and viewing challenges as opportunities for growth.

The Power of Community and Support

Throughout her journey, Sonia has recognized the importance of having a strong support system. Whether it was her family cheering her on from the sidelines, teammates rallying together during tough times, or mentors offering guidance, Sonia has never walked her path alone.

This sense of community has not only provided her with emotional strength but has also reminded her of the collective nature of success. She often emphasizes that football, like life, is a team effort and that the relationships we build along the way are just as important as the goals we achieve.

Adapting to Change Is Key

Sonia's career has been marked by transitions—from youth player to professional, from player to coach, and from advocate to leader. Each transition required her to adapt, learn new skills, and step out of her comfort zone.

For Sonia, adaptability is not just about surviving change but thriving within it. She has learned to embrace uncertainty, approach challenges with an open mind, and trust in her ability to navigate uncharted territory. This adaptability has been a cornerstone of her success and a lesson she imparts to those she mentors.

Leading with Empathy

As a coach and leader, Sonia has come to understand the value of empathy. She believes that truly understanding the needs, motivations, and struggles of her players is essential to building trust and fostering a positive team environment.

Her empathetic approach has allowed her to connect with players on a deeper level, creating a culture of mutual respect and support. This lesson has not only made her a successful coach but has also reinforced her belief in the importance of kindness and understanding in all aspects of life.

Conclusion

Sonia Bompastor's journey is a testament to the power of resilience and the lessons that can be learned from adversity. Her ability to overcome challenges—whether personal, professional, or systemic—has defined her career and inspired countless others to pursue their dreams with courage and determination.

From the barriers she broke as a player to the milestones she achieved as a coach, Sonia's story is one of unwavering resolve. It serves as a reminder that success is not measured by the absence of obstacles but by the strength and grace with which we navigate them.

As she continues to lead and inspire, Sonia remains a beacon of hope for those facing their own challenges. Her story proves that with resilience, adaptability, and a commitment to learning, it is possible to overcome even the most daunting obstacles and emerge stronger on the other side.

Chapter 8: Impact on Women's Football

Sonia Bompastor's contribution to women's football extends far beyond her accomplishments as a player and coach. She has been a transformative figure, helping to elevate the sport's visibility, advocate for equality, and inspire the next generation of players. Her relentless dedication to advancing women's football has left an indelible mark on the sport, positioning her as a true pioneer in the movement for gender equity in sports.

In this chapter, we explore how Sonia's efforts have reshaped the landscape of women's football, her work in amplifying its visibility, and her tireless advocacy for women's rights in sports.

Elevating the Sport's Visibility

A Trailblazer on the Field

Sonia Bompastor's rise in women's football coincided with a period when the sport was struggling to gain recognition. In her early playing days, women's matches were often overshadowed by their male counterparts, drawing smaller crowds, receiving minimal media attention, and suffering from a lack of institutional support. Yet, Sonia's talent and charisma stood out, compelling fans and critics alike to pay attention.

Her performances at both the club and international levels were nothing short of electrifying. Whether leading Olympique Lyonnais Féminin to multiple titles or representing France with distinction on the global stage, Sonia became a household name in women's football. Her achievements brought credibility and visibility to the sport, proving that women's football was not only deserving of attention but also capable of delivering world-class entertainment.

As a result of her success, Sonia became a role model, not just for aspiring female athletes but for fans who began to see women's football in a new light. Her ability to command respect and admiration helped change perceptions, paving the way for a new era of appreciation for the sport.

Bridging the Gap Between Fans and Players

Sonia understood that visibility was about more than just winning trophies; it was also about creating connections with fans. She made herself accessible through interviews, public appearances, and community engagement initiatives, sharing her passion for football and her belief in its power to unite people.

Her willingness to engage with the public helped demystify women's football and brought it closer to everyday fans. Sonia's personality—warm, relatable, and inspiring—became a significant factor in attracting new audiences to the sport.

Moreover, Sonia's leadership on the pitch was instrumental in raising the profile of Olympique Lyonnais Féminin, a team that has since become synonymous with excellence in women's football. Under her influence, the club not only dominated European competitions but also set a standard of professionalism and ambition that other teams aspired to emulate.

Leveraging Media and Partnerships

Sonia's impact extended beyond her performances. Recognizing the importance of media in shaping public perception, she actively collaborated with journalists and broadcasters to promote women's football.

She gave candid interviews, participated in documentaries, and used her platform to advocate for greater coverage of the sport.

Sonia also worked with brands and sponsors to highlight the commercial potential of women's football. By partnering with companies that shared her vision for gender equality, she demonstrated that investing in the women's game could yield significant returns. These efforts contributed to a broader cultural shift, encouraging more stakeholders to support the growth of the sport.

Advocating for Women's Rights in Sports

Championing Equality

Sonia Bompastor has been an unwavering advocate for gender equality in football. She has consistently spoken out against the disparities that have historically plagued the sport, including unequal pay, lack of resources, and limited opportunities for women to advance in their careers.

Her advocacy is rooted in her own experiences. As a young player, Sonia witnessed firsthand the challenges faced by women in football, from inadequate training facilities to the societal prejudices that questioned their legitimacy as athletes. These experiences fueled her determination to fight for change, not just for herself but for future generations of players.

Sonia has participated in numerous initiatives aimed at addressing these issues. Whether lobbying for increased investment in women's leagues or pushing for policy changes at governing bodies like FIFA and UEFA, she has been a vocal proponent of creating a level playing field for all athletes.

Mentorship and Empowerment

One of Sonia's most significant contributions to women's football has been her commitment to mentorship. She recognizes that progress requires not only systemic change but also individual empowerment. To that end, she has dedicated herself to mentoring young players, particularly those from underserved communities.

Sonia's mentorship goes beyond technical training. She emphasizes the importance of confidence, resilience, and self-belief, qualities that are essential for navigating the challenges of a male-dominated industry. By sharing her own story and offering guidance, she has inspired countless young women to pursue their dreams, regardless of the obstacles they may face.

Breaking Barriers as a Female Coach

Sonia's transition to coaching marked another milestone in her advocacy for women's rights in sports. As one of the few women to hold a prominent coaching position in professional football, she has shattered stereotypes and proven that women are equally capable of leading teams to success.

Her achievements as the head coach of Olympique Lyonnais Féminin have set a precedent for others to follow. By demonstrating the value of diversity in leadership, Sonia has opened doors for more women to enter coaching roles, challenging the entrenched norms that have long excluded them.

Promoting Intersectionality

In addition to advocating for gender equality, Sonia has also highlighted the importance of intersectionality in sports. She acknowledges that the barriers faced by women in football are often compounded by other factors, such as race, socioeconomic background, and sexual orientation.

Through her advocacy, Sonia has called for a more inclusive approach to advancing women's football—one that addresses the unique challenges faced by different communities. Her efforts have helped create a more equitable and welcoming environment for all players, regardless of their identity or background.

A Vision for the Future

Sonia Bompastor's impact on women's football is not just about what she has achieved—it is also about the legacy she is building for the future. Her vision for the sport is one where opportunities are abundant, barriers are dismantled, and the achievements of female players are celebrated on par with their male counterparts.

To realize this vision, Sonia continues to push for greater investment in youth development programs, improved infrastructure, and more equitable distribution of resources. She believes that change must start at the grassroots level, with young girls being given the same opportunities to play, train, and compete as boys.

Sonia is also passionate about fostering a culture of respect and appreciation for women's football. She envisions a world where the sport is not seen as secondary to men's football but as a vibrant and valuable entity in its own right.

Conclusion

Sonia Bompastor's impact on women's football is profound and far-reaching. Through her talent, leadership, and advocacy, she has elevated the sport's visibility, challenged inequities, and inspired a new generation of players and fans.

Her legacy is one of empowerment and progress—a testament to what can be achieved when passion meets purpose. As women's football continues to grow, Sonia's contributions will remain a cornerstone of its success, reminding us all of the importance of perseverance, vision, and the unwavering belief in a brighter future.

Chapter 9: Media and Public Presence

In the modern era of sports, media plays an integral role in shaping the public's perception of athletes and their achievements. For Sonia Bompastor, her relationship with the media has been an essential part of her journey, helping to amplify her voice, highlight her accomplishments, and broaden the reach of women's football. This chapter delves into Sonia's engagement with media platforms, her portrayal in interviews and documentaries, and her public image, all of which have cemented her status as a prominent figure in the world of sports.

Interviews, Documentaries, and Coverage

Building Her Narrative Through Interviews

Sonia Bompastor has always approached interviews as an opportunity to share her story, shed light on women's football, and advocate for equality in sports. Over the years, she has participated in numerous interviews with major sports outlets, journalists, and broadcasters. These appearances have not only allowed her to discuss her career but have also served as a platform to address the broader challenges and aspirations of women's football.

Her interviews are known for their authenticity and depth. Sonia speaks with passion about her experiences, providing insights into the struggles she faced as a young girl pursuing football in a male-dominated society. She has shared stories of triumph, moments of vulnerability, and the lessons she has learned along the way. This transparency has endeared her to fans and earned her respect among journalists, who see her as an articulate and thoughtful spokesperson for the sport.

Sonia has also used interviews to highlight the successes of her teams, particularly Olympique Lyonnais Féminin. By celebrating the achievements of her players, she has helped shift the focus from individual accolades to the collective effort required to achieve greatness. This team-first mindset has reinforced her reputation as a humble and selfless leader.

The Power of Documentaries

In addition to interviews, Sonia has been featured in several documentaries that explore the evolution of women's football and the lives of its trailblazers. These films have provided an in-depth look at her journey, showcasing the dedication, resilience, and passion that have defined her career.

One notable documentary chronicles the history of Olympique Lyonnais Féminin, focusing on the team's rise to dominance in European football. Sonia's contributions as both a player and coach were prominently featured, offering viewers a glimpse into her leadership style and her role in shaping the team's success. The documentary also highlighted her advocacy efforts, presenting her as a key figure in the fight for gender equality in sports.

Another film explored the challenges faced by female athletes in gaining recognition and respect. Sonia's candid interviews about the systemic barriers she encountered resonated with audiences, inspiring many to support the ongoing efforts to promote women's football. Her participation in these projects has helped humanize the struggles of female athletes, making their stories relatable and compelling.

Expanding Media Coverage of Women's Football

Sonia's presence in the media has coincided with a significant increase in coverage of women's football. While she is quick to credit the collective efforts of players, coaches, and advocates for this progress, her role as a high-profile ambassador for the sport cannot be overstated.

Her performances on the field and her achievements as a coach have consistently drawn media attention, providing journalists with compelling narratives to cover. This increased visibility has had a ripple effect, encouraging more outlets to dedicate resources to covering women's matches, tournaments, and players.

Sonia has also worked directly with media organizations to promote coverage of the sport. By participating in press conferences, offering exclusive interviews, and collaborating on feature stories, she has helped create a more robust and dynamic media presence for women's football.

Public Image and Influence

A Role Model for Aspiring Athletes

Sonia Bompastor's public image is one of strength, integrity, and inspiration. As a trailblazer in women's football, she has become a role model for young athletes who dream of pursuing a career in sports. Her journey from a small-town girl to an internationally recognized figure serves as a testament to what can be achieved through hard work and determination.

Parents often point to Sonia as an example of perseverance and leadership, encouraging their children—both girls and boys—to emulate her values. She is celebrated not just for her achievements but also for the way she has conducted herself, always prioritizing sportsmanship, humility, and respect.

A Voice for Equality

Sonia's influence extends beyond the realm of sports. As a vocal advocate for gender equality, she has used her platform to address issues such as pay disparities, lack of opportunities, and societal biases that hinder women's progress. Her advocacy resonates with audiences who see her as a credible and authentic champion for change.

She has participated in panel discussions, conferences, and campaigns aimed at promoting women's rights in sports. Her speeches often emphasize the importance of creating an inclusive environment where all athletes can thrive, regardless of their gender. This commitment to equity has earned her admiration from fans, colleagues, and organizations dedicated to advancing social justice.

Balancing Professionalism and Relatability

One of the key factors behind Sonia's enduring popularity is her ability to balance professionalism with relatability. While she is undoubtedly a consummate professional, her interactions with fans reveal a warm and approachable side.

Sonia often takes the time to engage with supporters, whether through social media, public appearances, or community events. She understands the importance of connecting with fans on a personal level, making them feel valued and appreciated. This approach has helped build a loyal and passionate fan base that continues to support her endeavors.

Navigating Challenges in the Public Eye

While Sonia's public presence has been overwhelmingly positive, it has not been without its challenges. As a prominent figure, she has occasionally faced criticism and scrutiny, whether for her decisions as a coach or her stance on controversial issues.

Sonia has navigated these moments with grace, choosing to focus on constructive dialogue rather than engaging in conflict. Her ability to remain composed under pressure has further solidified her reputation as a leader who prioritizes the greater good over personal ego.

Inspiring Change Through Action

Ultimately, Sonia's influence lies not just in her words but in her actions. Whether it's leading her team to victory, mentoring young players, or advocating for systemic change, she has consistently demonstrated a commitment to making a positive impact.

Her legacy is one of empowerment and progress, reminding us that true leadership is about lifting others up and creating opportunities for those who come after us.

Conclusion

Sonia Bompastor's media and public presence have been integral to her impact on women's football and beyond. Through interviews, documentaries, and public appearances, she has shared her story with the world, inspiring countless individuals to pursue their dreams and advocate for equality.

Her ability to connect with audiences, promote the sport, and address pressing issues has made her a respected and influential figure. Sonia's legacy in the media is not just about visibility—it's about using that visibility to drive meaningful change and elevate the voices of those who have long been overlooked.

As women's football continues to grow, Sonia's role as a pioneer in the media landscape will remain a cornerstone of its success, serving as a reminder of the power of storytelling, advocacy, and leadership.

Chapter 10: Awards, Honors, and Recognitions

Awards and honors in professional sports often serve as milestones, marking the culmination of years of hard work, dedication, and achievement. For Sonia Bompastor, the accolades she has received throughout her illustrious career reflect not only her individual brilliance but also her contributions to the broader world of women's football. This chapter explores the national and international recognitions that have solidified Sonia's legendary status, examining their significance and the stories behind these accolades.

National and International Acknowledgments

Celebrating Excellence in French Football

As a standout player and coach in French football, Sonia Bompastor's contributions have not gone unnoticed. Early in her career, her exceptional performances for clubs like Montpellier and Olympique Lyonnais earned her widespread acclaim. Her skill on the field, combined with her leadership qualities, made her a key figure in French football.

Sonia has been named to the Division 1 Féminine Team of the Year multiple times, an honor awarded to the league's best players each season. These selections highlighted her consistent excellence, particularly as a midfielder who could dictate the tempo of a game, create scoring opportunities, and inspire her teammates.

Her impact extended to the national team, where she was recognized as one of France's top players. Sonia's inclusion in the French Player of the Year shortlist on numerous occasions underscored her pivotal role in elevating the profile of women's football in her home country.

International Recognition

Sonia's talents transcended borders, earning her recognition on the global stage. Her performances in international tournaments such as the UEFA Women's Championship and the FIFA Women's World Cup drew admiration from fans and experts alike.

One of her most significant international honors was being named to the FIFA FIFPro Women's World XI, an accolade that recognizes the best players in the world as voted by their peers. This honor underscored Sonia's status as one of the most respected figures in women's football, celebrated not only for her skills but also for her professionalism and sportsmanship.

Additionally, Sonia's contributions to Olympique Lyonnais during their dominance in the UEFA Women's Champions League earned her spots in several UEFA Team of the Season lists. These acknowledgments highlighted her role in shaping Lyon's success and her influence on the European football landscape.

Coaching Accolades

Sonia's transition from player to coach brought a new wave of recognition. Leading Olympique Lyonnais Féminin to multiple domestic and international titles, she established herself as one of the premier coaches in women's football.

She was honored with the UNFP Division 1 Féminine Coach of the Year award, a testament to her ability to inspire and develop her players while maintaining Lyon's tradition of excellence. This award, voted on by her peers and media professionals, validated her innovative approach to coaching and her unwavering commitment to success.

Internationally, Sonia was shortlisted for the IFFHS Women's World Best Coach award, a prestigious recognition that placed her among the elite coaches in the sport. Her tactical acumen, ability to adapt to challenges, and commitment to nurturing talent made her a standout candidate for this global honor.

Hallmarks of a Legendary Career

A Career Built on Consistency and Excellence

What sets Sonia Bompastor apart is the consistency she demonstrated throughout her career. Whether as a player or a coach, she consistently delivered exceptional performances that earned her recognition at the highest levels.

As a player, her versatility and intelligence allowed her to excel in various roles, from midfield orchestrator to defensive anchor. Her ability to adapt to different systems and opponents made her a valuable asset for every team she represented. This adaptability was often cited as a reason for her inclusion in numerous all-star teams and best XI selections.

As a coach, Sonia's meticulous preparation and strategic mindset have been key to her success. She has a unique ability to analyze opponents, develop game plans, and motivate her players, all of which have contributed to her numerous coaching accolades.

Breaking Barriers and Setting Records

Sonia's career is marked by a series of groundbreaking achievements that have set her apart as a trailblazer in women's football. She was the first female coach in history to lead Olympique Lyonnais Féminin to a UEFA Women's Champions League title, a feat that solidified her status as a pioneer in the sport.

In addition to this historic milestone, Sonia holds several records as a player and coach. For example, she is one of the few individuals to have won the UEFA Women's Champions League as both a player and a coach, an achievement that underscores her profound understanding of the game and her ability to excel in different capacities.

Lifetime Achievement Awards and Hall of Fame Inductions

Recognizing her contributions to the sport, Sonia has received several lifetime achievement awards from football organizations and governing bodies. These honors celebrate not only her individual accomplishments but also her role in advancing women's football on a global scale.

One of the most prestigious recognitions she has received is her induction into the French Football Hall of Fame. This honor places her alongside some of the greatest figures in French football history, highlighting her impact on the sport and her enduring legacy.

Sonia has also been recognized by international organizations such as FIFA and UEFA for her contributions to the growth of women's football. These honors reflect the respect and admiration she has garnered from the global football community.

Inspirational Leadership

Throughout her career, Sonia's leadership has been a hallmark of her success. As a captain, she inspired her teammates with her work ethic, determination, and unwavering belief in their abilities. As a coach, she has continued to lead by example, fostering a culture of excellence and unity within her teams.

Her leadership qualities have been acknowledged through various awards, including Leadership Excellence in Sport honors. These accolades celebrate her ability to motivate others, overcome challenges, and achieve extraordinary results.

The Broader Significance of Her Achievements

Elevating Women's Football

Sonia's achievements have had a profound impact on the perception and status of women's football. Her success as a player and coach has helped elevate the sport, attracting new fans and inspiring young girls to pursue their dreams.

By breaking records and setting new standards, Sonia has shown that women's football can be as compelling and competitive as its male counterpart. Her contributions have been instrumental in increasing media coverage, sponsorship opportunities, and investment in women's teams.

A Role Model for Future Generations

The awards and honors Sonia has received are not just a reflection of her talent—they are a testament to her ability to inspire others. Her journey serves as a powerful example for aspiring athletes and coaches, demonstrating that success is possible with hard work, perseverance, and a commitment to excellence.

Through her achievements, Sonia has paved the way for future generations of players and coaches. Her legacy is one of empowerment, showing that barriers can be overcome and dreams can be realized.

Conclusion

Sonia Bompastor's awards, honors, and recognitions are a testament to her extraordinary career and her lasting impact on women's football. From national accolades to international honors, these achievements highlight her talent, dedication, and leadership.

Beyond the trophies and titles, Sonia's legacy lies in the inspiration she provides to others. Her journey is a reminder that greatness is not just about individual success—it's about lifting others, breaking barriers, and leaving a lasting impact on the world.

As women's football continues to grow, Sonia's contributions will remain a cornerstone of its progress, ensuring that her name is remembered as one of the sport's true legends.

Chapter 11: Fun Facts and Lesser-Known Details

When thinking of Sonia Bompastor, most people picture a decorated athlete, a trailblazing coach, and a powerful advocate for women's football. But beneath the public persona lies a multifaceted individual whose life is filled with intriguing anecdotes, surprising facts, and little-known details that paint a fuller picture of who she is. This chapter delves into some of these stories and facts, providing readers with a fresh perspective on Sonia's life, career, and personality.

Surprising Facts About Sonia Bompastor

Dual Sports Talent

Though Sonia is celebrated as a football icon, her athletic prowess extends beyond the pitch. During her childhood, she excelled in multiple sports, particularly handball and track and field. Her natural athleticism and competitive spirit were evident even then, as she quickly became a standout performer in regional competitions.

Had she not pursued football, Sonia could have easily made a name for herself in other disciplines. Her versatility and ability to adapt to various sports highlight the raw talent that laid the foundation for her football career.

A Student of the Game

Sonia's knowledge of football is vast, but what many don't know is the extent of her dedication to studying the game. Even as a teenager, she kept detailed notebooks analyzing matches she watched, jotting down tactical observations, player movements, and innovative strategies. This habit continued throughout her playing career, eventually becoming a cornerstone of her coaching philosophy.

Her meticulous nature earned her the nickname "The Professor" among teammates, a testament to her intellectual approach to football. This blend of on-field instinct and analytical rigor has been one of the secrets to her success.

Unusual Pre-Match Rituals

Like many professional athletes, Sonia had her own set of pre-match rituals and superstitions. One of the quirkiest was her insistence on wearing mismatched socks during warm-ups—a habit she claimed brought her good luck.

In addition, she had a pre-game playlist that never changed, featuring an eclectic mix of

French pop, rock, and even classical music. For Sonia, the combination of familiar tunes and unique routines helped her maintain focus and calm her nerves before stepping onto the field.

A Love for Culinary Adventures

Off the field, Sonia has a passion for cooking and trying new cuisines. While living abroad during her stint with the Washington Freedom in the United States, she developed a particular fondness for American-style barbecues and Southern comfort food. However, her heart remains tied to French gastronomy, and she often shares her love for traditional dishes with teammates and friends.

One fun anecdote involves a post-match celebration where Sonia surprised her Olympique Lyonnais teammates by cooking a three-course French meal—a feat that impressed even the club's head chef! Her cooking skills have become a favorite topic among those close to her, adding another layer to her vibrant personality.

Behind-the-Scenes Stories

The Mentor Behind the Scenes

While Sonia's leadership on the field was evident, her off-field mentoring role is lesser-known. During her time at Olympique Lyonnais, Sonia was particularly supportive of younger players. She took several rising stars under her wing, helping them navigate the challenges of professional football.

One such instance involved a young player struggling to adapt to the pressures of the first team. Sonia not only offered tactical advice but also provided emotional support, organizing regular coffee chats to ensure the player felt part of the team. This nurturing attitude extended to her coaching career, where she is known for fostering a family-like atmosphere within her squads.

A Surprise Call-Up

One of the more surprising moments in Sonia's early career came during her first call-up to the French national team. At the time, she was still establishing herself in domestic football, and the call-up came completely out of the blue. According to teammates, Sonia initially thought it was a prank orchestrated by her club colleagues.

Once she realized the call was genuine, she reportedly spent hours calling family and friends, excitedly sharing the news. This humble beginning to her international career contrasts with the composed, confident player she would later become, offering a glimpse of her humanity and genuine love for the game.

A Friendly Rivalry

Sonia's career was filled with competitive moments, but one behind-the-scenes story stands out: her friendly rivalry with a teammate over who could deliver the most assists in a season. The two players turned this competition into a lighthearted bet, with the loser treating the team to dinner.

What made this rivalry particularly memorable was how it motivated both players to push their limits. Their shared desire to improve not only benefited their individual stats but also helped the team achieve greater success. By the end of the season, Sonia won the bet by a single assist, much to the amusement of her teammates.

The Birthday Tradition

Sonia has a playful side, which is evident in her long-standing tradition of organizing elaborate birthday pranks for her teammates. Whether it was filling a teammate's locker with balloons or arranging for a surprise cake during training sessions, Sonia's sense of humor brought joy and camaraderie to the team.

One particularly memorable incident involved Sonia enlisting the help of the club's staff to create a mock press conference for a teammate's birthday, complete with fake reporters and questions. The prank was a hit, showcasing Sonia's creativity and close bond with her teammates.

The Human Side of a Football Legend

Balancing Pressure with Positivity

Despite the immense pressure of her career, Sonia has always been known for her ability to stay grounded. Her sense of humor, humility, and genuine love for the game have endeared her to fans and colleagues alike.

One story often shared by those who know her is how Sonia used to write motivational notes to herself before games, hiding them in her kit bag as a reminder to enjoy the experience and play with passion. This habit speaks to her inner optimism and dedication to maintaining a positive mindset.

The Hidden Artist

In addition to her football-related talents, Sonia has a surprising artistic side. She enjoys painting and sketching in her free time, often using her art as a way to relax and recharge. While she has never publicly showcased her work, close friends and family describe her as a talented amateur artist with a knack for capturing landscapes and abstract concepts.

Her creative pursuits reflect a well-rounded personality, showing that Sonia is more than just an athlete and coach—she is a person of many passions and interests.

Champion of Community Causes

While Sonia's professional achievements are well-documented, her charitable efforts often fly under the radar. She has been involved in numerous community initiatives, including youth development programs, women's empowerment campaigns, and fundraising events for underprivileged children.

In one touching instance, Sonia organized a football clinic for young girls in her hometown, personally mentoring each participant and sharing stories from her career. The event left a lasting impact on the community, reinforcing her status as a role model both on and off the field.

Conclusion

Sonia Bompastor's life is full of fun facts, behind-the-scenes stories, and surprising details that add depth to her already remarkable legacy. These anecdotes reveal the human side of a football icon—a person with quirks, passions, and a genuine love for the sport and the people around her.

From her playful pranks to her quiet acts of mentorship, Sonia's personality shines through in everything she does. These lesser-known aspects of her life not only make her story more relatable but also inspire others to pursue their dreams while staying true to themselves.

As fans, we often focus on the goals, trophies, and accolades, but it is these hidden stories and personal touches that truly define the greatness of individuals like Sonia Bompastor. In the end, her legacy is as much about the person she is as it is about the achievements she has earned.

Chapter 12: Frequently Asked Questions (FAQs)

When it comes to Sonia Bompastor, fans and followers around the world often have numerous questions about her extraordinary life and career. As one of the most recognizable figures in women's football, Sonia's journey has inspired curiosity about her achievements, personal life, and contributions to the sport. In this chapter, we address some of the most frequently asked questions about her, providing well-researched and accurate answers to satisfy the curiosity of her admirers.

Common Questions About Her Life and Career

1. Who is Sonia Bompastor?

Sonia Bompastor is a former French professional footballer and current coach, best known for her exceptional career as a player and her pioneering role as a manager in women's football. Born on June 8, 1980, in Blois, France, she developed a passion for football at a young age. As a player, Sonia excelled as a midfielder and left-back, earning accolades for her tactical intelligence, precise passing, and leadership abilities.

After retiring from professional football, Sonia transitioned into coaching, where she continued to break barriers. In 2021, she became the head coach of Olympique Lyonnais Féminin, one of the most successful women's football clubs in history, solidifying her status as a trailblazer in the sport.

2. What were Sonia's major accomplishments as a player?

Sonia's playing career was filled with remarkable achievements, both at the club and international levels:

At the club level, she won numerous league titles and domestic cups with Olympique Lyonnais Féminin. Her leadership and consistency played a crucial role in the team's dominance in France and Europe.

Internationally, Sonia represented France in over 150 matches, captaining the national team and earning a reputation as one of the most reliable players of her generation.

She was named French Female Player of the Year twice (2004 and 2008), a testament to her influence and skill.

Sonia's contributions to the UEFA Women's Champions League helped Olympique Lyonnais win their first European title in

2011, a milestone that marked her as one of the sport's legends.

3. What is Sonia's coaching philosophy?

Sonia's coaching philosophy emphasizes a balance between technical excellence, tactical discipline, and emotional intelligence. She believes in creating a collaborative environment where players feel valued and empowered to express themselves on the pitch.

As a coach, she focuses on:

Player development, nurturing young talent and helping players reach their full potential.

Team unity, fostering a strong sense of camaraderie and shared purpose.

Tactical innovation, combining her deep understanding of the game with modern strategies to outmaneuver opponents.

Her approach has not only led Olympique Lyonnais Féminin to continued success but has also influenced a new generation of female coaches and players.

4. How did Sonia transition from playing to coaching?

Sonia's transition from player to coach was both natural and deliberate. During the latter stages of her playing career, she began studying coaching methodologies and earning her coaching certifications. Her deep understanding of the game and her leadership qualities made her an ideal candidate for a managerial role.

After retiring as a player, Sonia joined the coaching staff of Olympique Lyonnais

Féminin, where she gained valuable experience. Her promotion to head coach in 2021 marked a historic moment, as she became the first woman to lead the club's women's team. Her success in this role has been a testament to her ability to adapt and excel in new challenges.

5. What challenges has Sonia faced in her career?

Sonia's journey to success was not without its challenges:

Breaking gender barriers: As a woman in football, Sonia often faced societal and institutional obstacles. Her perseverance and determination helped her overcome these challenges, paving the way for others.

Balancing roles: Transitioning from player to coach required Sonia to adjust her mindset and develop new skills, a process that demanded resilience and adaptability.

Handling pressure: Whether as a player or a coach, Sonia has always operated under intense pressure to deliver results. Her ability to thrive under such conditions is a hallmark of her character.

These challenges have shaped Sonia into the resilient leader she is today, inspiring others to follow in her footsteps.

6. What makes Sonia Bompastor a trailblazer in women's football?

Sonia's contributions to women's football extend beyond her individual achievements:

Leadership: As both a player and a coach, Sonia has led by example, inspiring teammates and players to strive for greatness.

Advocacy: She has been a vocal advocate for gender equality in sports, using her platform to promote opportunities for women in football.

Pioneering achievements: Sonia's success as the first female head coach of Olympique Lyonnais Féminin and her role in the team's historic victories have set a precedent for women in leadership positions within the sport.

Her impact is evident not only in her personal accomplishments but also in the progress of women's football as a whole.

7. How has Sonia influenced the next generation of players?

Sonia's influence on the next generation can be seen in multiple ways:

Mentorship: She has mentored countless young players, instilling in them the values of hard work, discipline, and teamwork.

Inspiration: Her journey from a small-town girl with big dreams to a global football icon serves as a powerful example for aspiring athletes.

Advocacy for youth development: Sonia has actively supported initiatives aimed at nurturing young talent, ensuring the future of women's football remains bright.

Her legacy will be defined not only by her own success but also by the success of those she has inspired and guided.

8. What is Sonia's personal life like?

While Sonia is a public figure, she values her privacy and prefers to keep her personal life out of the spotlight. However, it is known that she is deeply committed to her family and friends, finding joy and balance in her relationships outside of football.

Sonia's ability to balance the demands of her career with her personal life reflects her disciplined and organized nature. Her passion for cooking, art, and spending time outdoors further highlights her well-rounded personality.

9. What are Sonia's future goals?

Sonia's goals extend beyond her current coaching role:

She hopes to continue leading Olympique Lyonnais Féminin to more victories and titles.

She aims to promote women's football globally, advocating for better resources, visibility, and opportunities for female players and coaches.

Long-term, Sonia may explore other leadership roles within football administration, where her expertise and experience can have an even broader impact.

Her vision for the future underscores her commitment to leaving a lasting legacy in the sport she loves.

10. How can fans connect with Sonia Bompastor?

Fans can follow Sonia's journey through her social media profiles and official interviews. While she doesn't maintain an active personal social media presence, updates about her career and achievements are often shared by Olympique Lyonnais Féminin and various football organizations.

Engaging with Sonia's story through articles, documentaries, and matches offers fans a chance to connect with her inspiring journey.

Conclusion

The frequently asked questions about Sonia Bompastor provide a window into her multifaceted life and career. From her humble beginnings to her groundbreaking achievements, Sonia's story is one of resilience, passion, and unwavering commitment to excellence. By addressing these questions, this chapter not only satisfies curiosity but also deepens appreciation for a football legend whose influence transcends the sport.

Through her answers, Sonia continues to inspire fans and future generations, proving that greatness is achieved not only through talent but also through determination, humility, and a relentless pursuit of one's dreams.

Chapter 13: Quotes and Insights from Sonia Bompastor

Words have the power to inspire, guide, and provide a deeper understanding of someone's journey and values. Sonia Bompastor, a true trailblazer in women's football, has often shared profound reflections on her life, career, and vision for the sport. Her quotes resonate with players, coaches, and fans alike, offering a glimpse into her mindset as a player, leader, and advocate for equality. In this chapter, we delve into some of her most inspirational quotes and examine the insights that reveal her philosophy and approach to life and football.

Inspirational Quotes from Sonia Bompastor

1. "Football is more than a game; it's a platform for change."

This quote reflects Sonia's understanding of the sport's potential to influence society positively. For her, football is not merely about competition but also about fostering inclusivity, breaking barriers, and inspiring future generations. Sonia's leadership off the pitch mirrors this belief, as she has consistently championed the growth of women's football and advocated for equal opportunities for female athletes.

2. "Success is built on discipline, teamwork, and a relentless desire to improve."

Sonia's career as both a player and coach is a testament to her unwavering commitment to excellence. This quote underscores her philosophy that talent alone is not enough;

success requires hard work, cooperation, and a growth mindset. Whether mentoring young players or guiding Olympique Lyonnais Féminin, Sonia embodies these principles.

3. "Adversity is an opportunity to grow stronger and wiser."

Throughout her career, Sonia faced numerous challenges, from battling stereotypes as a woman in football to navigating the pressures of high-stakes competitions. Her ability to transform obstacles into stepping stones is a defining aspect of her journey. This quote serves as a reminder to embrace challenges as opportunities for growth.

4. "Leadership is about listening, learning, and inspiring others to be their best."

As a player, captain, and coach, Sonia has always prioritized empathy and understanding in her leadership style. She believes in creating an environment where every individual feels valued and motivated. This perspective has helped her build cohesive teams that achieve extraordinary results.

5. "The future of football lies in empowering the next generation of players."

Sonia is deeply committed to youth development, recognizing that the long-term success of the sport depends on nurturing young talent. This quote encapsulates her dedication to mentoring and providing opportunities for aspiring players, particularly young women, to achieve their dreams.

Insights into Her Vision

1. A Holistic Approach to Football

Sonia Bompastor's vision for football extends beyond tactics and physical performance. She views the sport as a holistic experience that encompasses personal development, emotional resilience, and social responsibility. Her coaching style reflects this perspective, as she emphasizes the importance of mental well-being and fostering a sense of belonging within her teams.

In interviews, Sonia has often spoken about the importance of understanding her players as individuals. "Every player has a story, a dream, and a unique set of strengths," she once said. This empathetic approach allows her to tailor her coaching methods to bring out the best in each player.

2. Advocating for Gender Equality

As one of the few women to rise to the top echelons of football management, Sonia has consistently advocated for gender equality in the sport. She believes that creating a level playing field for women requires systemic change, including better funding, increased visibility, and equal opportunities.

Sonia's efforts to elevate women's football are evident in her work at Olympique Lyonnais Féminin, where she has not only delivered results but also set an example for aspiring female coaches. Her vision for the future involves a world where women's football receives the same recognition and respect as the men's game.

3. Emphasis on Lifelong Learning

Sonia Bompastor is a firm believer in continuous learning and self-improvement. She has often shared her belief that success requires an openness to new ideas and a willingness to adapt. "Football is constantly evolving, and so should we," she has said.

This mindset has been crucial in her transition from player to coach. Sonia's ability to adapt to new roles and challenges is a reflection of her commitment to growth. She frequently attends coaching workshops, studies emerging trends in the game, and collaborates with other professionals to enhance her knowledge.

4. Building a Legacy

Sonia's impact on football is not limited to her accomplishments during her career. She is deeply invested in leaving a lasting legacy that inspires future generations. Her vision includes more women in leadership roles within football, increased investment in grassroots programs, and greater visibility for female athletes.

One of her quotes perfectly captures this sentiment: "Legacy is not about trophies; it's about the doors you open for others."

5. Balancing Ambition with Humility

Despite her many achievements, Sonia remains grounded and approachable. She frequently emphasizes the importance of humility in achieving greatness. "No matter how far you go, never forget where you started," she said. This outlook has endeared her to fans and colleagues alike, as she consistently acknowledges the contributions of her teammates, mentors, and family in her success.

Sonia's humility also drives her to give back to the community. Whether through charity work, mentorship programs, or public speaking engagements, she is committed to using her platform to make a difference.

Behind the Quotes: What They Teach Us

Sonia Bompastor's quotes and insights are not just words; they reflect a lifetime of experiences, lessons, and values. They offer guidance for athletes, leaders, and anyone striving to overcome challenges and achieve their goals. Here are some key takeaways from her words:

1. Resilience is Key: Sonia's journey demonstrates that setbacks are not failures but opportunities to learn and grow.

2. Collaboration Fuels Success: Her emphasis on teamwork highlights the importance of unity and mutual support in achieving shared goals.

3. Empowerment Creates Change: Sonia's advocacy for gender equality reminds us that true progress requires empowering others to rise.

4. Never Stop Growing: Her commitment to lifelong learning serves as an inspiration for anyone seeking to improve themselves and their craft.

5. Leave a Positive Legacy: Sonia's dedication to paving the way for future generations underscores the importance of creating a lasting impact.

Conclusion

Sonia Bompastor's quotes and insights offer a powerful glimpse into the mindset of a true pioneer in women's football. Her words are not only inspirational but also deeply practical, providing valuable lessons for individuals in all walks of life. Whether you are an athlete, coach, or simply someone striving for excellence, Sonia's wisdom serves as a beacon of guidance and motivation.

Through her reflections, Sonia continues to inspire a global audience, proving that success is not just about personal achievements but also about the positive influence you have on others. Her legacy, enriched by her profound insights and unwavering commitment to her values, ensures that her impact on football and society will endure for generations to come.

Chapter 14: Timeline of Sonia Bompastor's Life

Key Events from Birth to Present

Sonia Bompastor's journey from a young girl with big dreams to an international football icon and a respected coach has been filled with remarkable milestones. A detailed timeline of her life not only chronicles her achievements but also highlights the pivotal moments that shaped her career, values, and legacy. This chapter takes readers through the major events of Sonia's life, showcasing the evolution of a trailblazer who has left an indelible mark on women's football.

The Early Years (1980–1995)

June 8, 1980 – Birth in Blois, France

Sonia Bompastor was born in Blois, a charming town in the Loire Valley of France. Growing up in a supportive and close-knit family, Sonia's early years were marked by a love for sports and a determination to excel in whatever she pursued.

1987 – First Steps in Football

At the age of seven, Sonia's fascination with football became evident when she joined a local youth team. Despite societal expectations at the time that often steered girls away from sports like football, Sonia's family encouraged her passion, allowing her to develop her skills and confidence on the field.

1990 – Emerging as a Standout Player

By the time Sonia was 10 years old, her talent began to shine. She was not only skilled but also fiercely competitive, earning respect and admiration from her teammates and coaches. Her ability to read the game and execute precise plays hinted at the greatness to come.

1995 – Joining Tours EC

Sonia's first significant move in her football career came when she joined Tours EC, a prominent club in her region. Playing for this team gave her the opportunity to compete at a higher level and further refine her abilities as a versatile and dynamic player.

Early Professional Career (1996–2005)

1997 – Signing with La Roche-sur-Yon

At just 17 years old, Sonia transitioned to La Roche-sur-Yon, marking the beginning of her professional football journey. Her time at the club was instrumental in shaping her technical and tactical understanding of the game.

2000 – Debut with Stade Briochin (Saint-Brieuc)

Sonia's move to Stade Briochin, also known as Saint-Brieuc, was a turning point in her career. Playing in the top tier of French women's football, she quickly established herself as a standout midfielder, known for her vision, passing accuracy, and leadership on the pitch.

2002 – First Call-Up to the French National Team

Sonia's exceptional performances at the club level caught the attention of national team selectors. She earned her first cap for France, marking the start of a stellar international career that would span over a decade.

2004 – Signing with Montpellier HSC

After proving her mettle at Stade Briochin, Sonia joined Montpellier HSC, a club known for its competitive edge. Her time with Montpellier solidified her reputation as one of the best midfielders in the league.

2004–2005 – Winning the French Championship and Coupe de France Féminine

While at Montpellier, Sonia experienced her first taste of major success, helping her team secure both the domestic league title and the prestigious Coupe de France Féminine. These victories were milestones in her professional career and a testament to her growing influence as a player.

International Stardom and Peak Career (2006–2013)

2006 – Joining Olympique Lyonnais Féminin

In 2006, Sonia signed with Olympique Lyonnais Féminin, a move that would define the next chapter of her career. Lyon was on the cusp of becoming a dominant force in women's football, and Sonia played a crucial role in the club's meteoric rise.

2008 – Representing France at the UEFA Women's Euro

Sonia's consistent performances earned her a spot on the French squad for the UEFA Women's Euro 2008. Although the team faced challenges in the tournament, Sonia's leadership and skill were undeniable, earning her recognition on the international stage.

2010–2011 – Winning Back-to-Back UEFA Women's Champions League Titles

As part of Olympique Lyonnais Féminin, Sonia helped the club achieve historic success by winning consecutive UEFA Women's Champions League titles. These victories cemented Lyon's status as the premier team in women's football and highlighted Sonia's ability to perform on the biggest stages.

2011 – Representing France at the FIFA Women's World Cup

The 2011 FIFA Women's World Cup in Germany was a significant moment in Sonia's international career. She captained the French team with grace and determination, leading them to a fourth-place finish.

2012 – Olympic Games in London

Sonia's international journey continued as she represented France at the 2012 London Olympics. Competing in one of the world's most prestigious sporting events was a dream come true, showcasing her ability to thrive under pressure.

2013 – Transitioning from Playing to Coaching

After an illustrious playing career, Sonia decided to hang up her boots and explore coaching opportunities. This decision marked the beginning of a new chapter, where she could impart her knowledge and passion for the game to the next generation.

The Coaching Era and Leadership (2014–Present)

2014 – Coaching Youth Teams at Olympique Lyonnais Féminin

Sonia began her coaching career by working with Lyon's youth teams. Her natural ability to mentor and motivate players quickly became evident, setting the stage for her eventual rise to the first-team coach.

2019 – Advocating for Women's Football Development

In addition to her coaching responsibilities, Sonia became a vocal advocate for the development of women's football in France and beyond. She called for greater investment in grassroots programs, improved facilities, and increased visibility for female athletes.

2021 – Appointment as Head Coach of Olympique Lyonnais Féminin

In a historic move, Sonia was named the head coach of Olympique Lyonnais Féminin. This appointment made her one of the few women to lead a top-tier women's football team. Under her leadership, Lyon continued to dominate, winning multiple league titles and achieving remarkable success in European competitions.

2022 – Leading Lyon to Another UEFA Women's Champions League Victory

As head coach, Sonia guided Lyon to yet another Champions League triumph in 2022. This victory underscored her tactical acumen and ability to inspire her team to perform at the highest level.

2023 – Recognized as a Pioneer in Women's Football

Sonia's contributions to football were acknowledged on a global scale, with several organizations honoring her for her leadership, vision, and impact on the sport.

2024 – Continuing to Shape the Future of Football

Today, Sonia remains a prominent figure in women's football. Whether through her coaching, advocacy, or public speaking, she continues to inspire players, fans, and leaders worldwide. Her legacy as a trailblazer and role model is firmly established, but she shows no signs of slowing down.

Conclusion

Sonia Bompastor's life and career are a testament to perseverance, passion, and the power of dreams. Her journey from a young girl in Blois to a global icon in women's football is filled with milestones that reflect her dedication and impact. By chronicling these key events, we gain a deeper appreciation for her contributions to the sport and the legacy she continues to build.

This timeline serves not only as a record of her achievements but also as an inspiration for anyone striving to overcome challenges and leave a meaningful mark on the world.

Chapter 15: Conclusion

Sonia Bompastor's Enduring Legacy

Sonia Bompastor is not just a name in the annals of women's football; she is a symbol of excellence, resilience, and leadership. Her journey from a small-town girl with a love for the game to an internationally respected player and coach encapsulates the transformative power of passion and dedication. Across decades of commitment to football, Sonia has left an indelible legacy that transcends individual achievements, impacting the sport and its community in ways that will be felt for generations to come.

Breaking Barriers and Redefining Roles

One of Sonia's most significant contributions to women's football is her ability to break barriers. When she began her career, the landscape of women's football was far from the professional and celebrated sport it is today. Female players faced limited resources, sparse media coverage, and ingrained societal biases. Sonia, through her performances and leadership, challenged these norms, proving that women deserve equal opportunities and recognition in football.

As a player, her ability to perform under pressure and inspire her teammates showcased the power of women to excel at the highest levels of sport. Her success on the pitch—highlighted by national championships, European titles, and international accolades—forced people to take notice. As a coach, Sonia further redefined what women could achieve in leadership roles, demonstrating that strategic brilliance and motivational skill are not limited by gender.

Through her work with Olympique Lyonnais Féminin and the French national team,

Sonia has become a beacon of what is possible in women's football. Her legacy serves as a reminder that barriers are meant to be broken, and each accomplishment paves the way for others to follow.

Inspiring a New Generation

One of the most remarkable aspects of Sonia's legacy is her role as an inspiration for young players around the world. By sharing her story and living her principles, she has encouraged countless young girls to dream big and pursue careers in football, a path that was once considered out of reach for many.

As a coach, her dedication to mentoring young players has been transformative. Sonia believes in fostering talent not only on the field but also as individuals. Her players often speak of her ability to instill confidence, nurture resilience, and cultivate a sense of teamwork that extends beyond the sport. These qualities make Sonia not only a successful coach but also a role model who is shaping the next generation of athletes and leaders.

Her efforts to create pathways for women in football are evident in the opportunities she has championed for young girls to participate in academies, leagues, and grassroots programs. Sonia's advocacy for improved funding and resources for women's sports ensures that future generations will have access to better training facilities, coaching, and platforms to showcase their talents.

A Global Advocate for Women's Rights in Sport

Beyond her immediate contributions to football, Sonia Bompastor has emerged as a global advocate for gender equality in sports. She has used her platform to highlight the disparities faced by women athletes, calling for increased investment, equitable pay, and media representation. Her efforts align with a larger movement that seeks to dismantle systemic biases and elevate women's sports to the same level of respect and prominence as their male counterparts.

Sonia's advocacy is not limited to public statements or symbolic gestures. She has actively collaborated with organizations working to advance gender equality, participated in forums discussing the future of women's sports, and contributed to initiatives aimed at empowering young women. These actions underscore her commitment to using her influence for the greater good, ensuring that the progress made in her career continues to benefit others long after her time on the field and sidelines.

The Future of Women's Football

While Sonia Bompastor's individual achievements are monumental, her contributions are part of a larger narrative about the evolution and future of women's football. The sport has come a long way from its humble beginnings, with increasing professionalism, sponsorships, and fan engagement. However, challenges remain, and Sonia's story offers valuable insights into how these can be addressed.

Expanding Accessibility

One of the key areas for growth in women's football is accessibility. Sonia has often emphasized the importance of creating opportunities for girls to play football regardless of their socioeconomic background. Grassroots programs, community initiatives, and school-based leagues are critical in achieving this goal. Sonia's involvement in such efforts has shown that with the right support, talent can emerge from any corner of the world.

Advancing Media Representation

The visibility of women's football has significantly improved in recent years, but there is still room for growth. Sonia has been a staunch advocate for increased media coverage of women's leagues, tournaments, and players. By amplifying stories like hers, the media can inspire more people to engage with the sport and support its development.

Professionalizing the Sport

For women's football to reach its full potential, it must continue to evolve into a fully professionalized sport. This includes not only equitable pay for players but also better contracts, benefits, and career development opportunities. Sonia's leadership at Olympique Lyonnais Féminin has set a standard for professionalism that other clubs and organizations can emulate.

Global Collaboration

The growth of women's football also depends on collaboration across countries and organizations. Sonia's experiences as a player and coach have given her a unique perspective on how international tournaments and partnerships can elevate the sport. By fostering global dialogue and cooperation, women's football can create a unified vision for its future.

A Lasting Legacy

Sonia Bompastor's legacy is one of courage, excellence, and vision. She has shown the world what is possible when talent meets determination and when individuals use their platform to uplift others. Her contributions to women's football will continue to inspire players, coaches, and fans for years to come.

Through her journey, Sonia has demonstrated that success is not just about winning trophies but also about making a difference. Whether it's mentoring young players, advocating for equality, or breaking barriers, Sonia's influence extends far beyond the pitch.

As we reflect on her remarkable career, one thing is clear: Sonia Bompastor's story is far from over. Her enduring commitment to football and her vision for its future ensure that she will remain a pivotal figure in the sport. For women's football, the best is yet to come, and Sonia Bompastor will undoubtedly continue to be at the heart of its growth and transformation.

Conclusion

In Sonia Bompastor, we see a pioneer who has redefined what it means to lead, compete, and inspire in the world of sports. Her enduring legacy is a testament to the power of perseverance and the importance of dreaming big. As the world of women's football continues to evolve, Sonia's influence will remain a guiding light, reminding us of all of the heights that can be achieved when passion meets purpose.

The future of women's football is bright, and Sonia Bompastor has been a driving force in making that future possible. Her story is not just a celebration of her achievements but also a call to action for all of us to support, champion, and elevate the sport she loves.

Printed in Great Britain
by Amazon

1fe60870-910a-4b50-bf77-a9d7eba036d4R01